CW00661421

by Iain Gray

PUBLISHING

WRITING *to* REMEMBER

WRITING *to* REMEMBER

79 Main Street, Newtongrange,
Midlothian EH22 4NA
Tel: 0131 344 0414   Fax: 0845 075 6085
E-mail: info@lang-syne.co.uk
www.langsyneshop.co.uk

Design by Dorothy Meikle
Printed by Printwell Ltd
© Lang Syne Publishers Ltd 2016

ISBN 978-1-85217-592-4

Martin

MOTTOES include:
Sure and steadfast
(and)
My help is from the Lord.

CRESTS include:
A Talbot's head
(and)
A starfish.

NAME variations include:
Martyn
Matin
Mattin

Chapter one:

The origins of popular surnames

by George Forbes and Iain Gray

If you don't know where you came from, you won't know where you're going is a frequently quoted observation and one that has a particular resonance today when there has been a marked upsurge in interest in genealogy, with increasing numbers of people curious to trace their family roots.

Main sources for genealogical research include census returns and official records of births, marriages and deaths – and the key to unlocking the detail they contain is obviously a family surname, one that has been 'inherited' and passed from generation to generation.

No matter our station in life, we all have a surname – but it was not until about the middle of the fourteenth century that the practice of being identified by a particular surname became commonly established throughout the British Isles.

Previous to this, it was normal for a person to be identified through the use of only a forename.

But as population gradually increased and there were many more people with the same forename, surnames were adopted to distinguish one person, or community, from another.

Many common English surnames are patronymic in origin, meaning they stem from the forename of one's father – with 'Johnson,' for example, indicating 'son of John.'

It was the Normans, in the wake of their eleventh century conquest of Anglo-Saxon England, a pivotal moment in the nation's history, who first brought surnames into usage – although it was a gradual process.

For the Normans, these were names initially based on the title of their estates, local villages and chateaux in France to distinguish and identify these landholdings.

Such grand descriptions also helped enhance the prestige of these warlords and generally glorify their lofty positions high above the humble serfs slaving away below in the pecking order who had only single names, often with Biblical connotations as in Pierre and Jacques.

The only descriptive distinctions among the peasantry concerned their occupations, like 'Pierre the swineherd' or 'Jacques the ferryman.'

Roots of surnames that came into usage in England not only included Norman-French, but also Old French, Old Norse, Old English, Middle English, German, Latin, Greek, Hebrew and the Gaelic languages of the Celts.

The Normans themselves were originally Vikings, or 'Northmen', who raided, colonised and eventually settled down around the French coastline.

The had sailed up the Seine in their longboats in 900AD under their ferocious leader Rollo and ruled the roost in north eastern France before sailing over to conquer England in 1066 under Duke William of Normandy – better known to posterity as William the Conqueror, or King William I of England.

Granted lands in the newly-conquered England, some of their descendants later acquired territories in Wales, Scotland and Ireland – taking not only their own surnames, but also the practice of adopting a surname, with them.

But it was in England where Norman rule and custom first impacted, particularly in relation to the adoption of surnames.

This is reflected in the famous *Domesday Book*, a massive survey of much of England and Wales, ordered by William I, to determine who owned what, what it was worth and therefore how much they were liable to pay in taxes to the voracious Royal Exchequer.

Completed in 1086 and now held in the National Archives in Kew, London, 'Domesday' was an Old English word meaning 'Day of Judgement.'

This was because, in the words of one contemporary chronicler, "its decisions, like those of the Last Judgement, are unalterable."

It had been a requirement of all those English landholders – from the richest to the poorest – that they identify themselves for the purposes of the survey and for future reference by means of a surname.

This is why the *Domesday Book*, although written in Latin as was the practice for several centuries with both civic and ecclesiastical records, is an invaluable source for the early appearance of a wide range of English surnames.

Several of these names were coined in connection with occupations.

These include Baker and Smith, while Cooks, Chamberlains, Constables and Porters were to be found carrying out duties in large medieval households.

The church's influence can be found in names such as Bishop, Friar and Monk while the popular name of Bennett derives from the late fifth to mid-sixth century Saint Benedict, founder of the Benedictine order of monks.

The early medical profession is represented by Barber, while businessmen produced names that include Merchant and Sellers.

Down at the village watermill, the names that cropped up included Millar/Miller, Walker and Fuller, while other self-explanatory trades included Cooper, Tailor, Mason and Wright.

Even the scenery was utilised as in Moor, Hill, Wood and Forrest – while the hunt and the chase supplied names that include Hunter, Falconer, Fowler and Fox.

Colours are also a source of popular surnames, as in Black, Brown, Gray/Grey, Green and White, and would have denoted the colour of the clothing the person habitually wore or, apart from the obvious exception of 'Green', one's hair colouring or even complexion.

The surname Red developed into Reid, while

Blue was rare and no-one wanted to be associated with yellow.

Rather self-important individuals took surnames that include Goodman and Wiseman, while physical attributes crept into surnames such as Small and Little.

Many families proudly boast the heraldic device known as a Coat of Arms, as featured on our front cover.

The central motif of the Coat of Arms would originally have been what was borne on the shield of a warrior to distinguish himself from others on the battlefield.

Not featured on the Coat of Arms, but high-lighted on page three, is the family motto and related crest – with the latter frequently different from the central motif.

Adding further variety to the rich cultural heritage that is represented by surnames is the appearance in recent times in lists of the 100 most common names found in England of ones that include Khan, Patel and Singh – names that have proud roots in the vast sub-continent of India.

Echoes of a far distant past can still be found in our surnames and they can be borne with pride in commemoration of our forebears.

Chapter two:

Wars of conquest

Bearers of the surname of Martin can lay claim to rather warlike origins, in the form of Mars, the feared Roman god of war, from whom the name is derived through the Latin form of 'Martinus.'

The champion of military power and conquest, Mars also had a more peaceful aspect as a protector of farmers, while his son Romulus is believed in legend to have built the walls of Rome.

A popular forename from earliest times, it increased in popularity in the early Christian era through veneration of the fourth century St Martin of Tours and, in common with many other forenames, or Christian names, was also gradually adopted as a surname.

In Ireland, meanwhile, the name is an Anglicised version of the ancient Irish-Gaelic 'Mairtine', a tribe of Celtic roots.

Many surnames such as Martin were introduced to England in the wake of the Norman Conquest of 1066, a pivotal event in the nation's history.

By this date, Anglo-Saxon England had become a nation with several powerful competitors to the throne.

In what were extremely complex family, political and military machinations, the king was Harold II, who had succeeded to the throne following the death of Edward the Confessor.

But his right to the throne was contested by two powerful competitors – his brother-in-law King Harold Hardrada of Norway, in alliance with Tostig, Harold II's brother, and Duke William II of Normandy.

In what has become known as The Year of Three Battles, Hardrada invaded England and gained victory over the English king on September 20 at the battle of Fulford, in Yorkshire.

Five days later, however, Harold II decisively defeated his brother-in-law and brother at the battle of Stamford Bridge.

But he had little time to celebrate his victory, having to immediately march south from Yorkshire to encounter a mighty invasion force, led by Duke William of Normandy, that had landed at Hastings, in East Sussex.

Harold's battle-hardened but exhausted force of Anglo-Saxon soldiers confronted the Normans on

October 14 in a battle subsequently depicted on the Bayeux tapestry – a 23ft. long strip of embroidered linen thought to have been commissioned eleven years after the event by the Norman Odo of Bayeux.

Harold drew up a strong defensive position at the top of Senlac Hill, building a shield wall to repel Duke William's cavalry and infantry.

The Normans suffered heavy losses, but through a combination of the deadly skill of their archers and the ferocious determination of their cavalry they eventually won the day.

Anglo-Saxon morale had collapsed on the battlefield as word spread through the ranks that Harold had been killed – the Bayeux Tapestry depicting this as having happened when he was struck by an arrow to the head.

Amidst the carnage of the battlefield, it was difficult to identify him – the last of the Anglo-Saxon kings.

William was declared King of England on December 25, and the complete subjugation of his Anglo-Saxon subjects followed.

Those Normans who had fought on his behalf were rewarded with the lands of Anglo-Saxons, many of whom sought exile abroad as mercenaries.

Within an astonishingly short space of time, Norman manners, customs and law were imposed on England – laying the basis for what subsequently became established 'English' custom and practice.

A prominent Norman family of the Martin name, originally in the form of 'fitz Martin', are believed to have first introduced it as a surname to England after being granted lands in Leicestershire, as reward for their service to William.

In the decades following the entrenchment of the Normans in their English landholdings, meanwhile, they became known as Anglo-Normans, and one prominent family of Anglo-Norman Martins came to hold lands in Somerset, Dorset and Devon.

It was through his brother-in-law William de Courcy and his grandfather Serlo de Burci that the Anglo-Norman knight Robert fitz Martin, or Martin, came to inherit these lands.

But the acquisition of further rich territory was to follow through his support for Henry I in suppressing rebellion against his power that had broken out in Wales.

With Norman holdings in Wales under threat, Henry mustered a formidable force of three armies in

1114 to crush the rebellion, and among their mail-clad ranks was the ambitious and warlike Martin.

The rebellion was indeed crushed, through sheer military might, and as reward for his support, Henry granted Martin the barony of Cemais, located between Cardigan and Fishguard and now part of modern-day Pembrokeshire.

Shortly after obtaining the barony, Martin and his wife Maude Peveril founded St Dogmael's Abbey, near Cardigan, for monks of the Tironsensian Order.

But in what is known as The Great Revolt of 1136 to 1137, Wales was convulsed yet again by rebellion and much of Cemais reclaimed by the native Welsh.

An army of Normans, who included Martin, was engaged by a rebel force led by Rhys ap Gruffyd and other prominent Welsh leaders at the battle of Crug Mawr – a hill in the Black Mountains in Powys, and were routed.

So panicked was the rout that, trying to cross a bridge at the River Teifi, the flimsy structure broke under their weight and hundreds are reported to have drowned.

The surviving fugitives managed to reach the

town of Cardigan and, despite it being taken and burned by the rebels, Martin managed to defend Cardigan Castle until the rebellion was finally quelled.

His military prowess came to the fore again during the period known as The Anarchy – a bloody civil war that raged until 1154 between Henry I's successor to the throne, Stephen, who was a grandson of William I, and Henry's daughter, the Empress Matilda.

Martin, who had steadfastly supported Matilda, died in about 1159, while his former territory of Cemais was eventually regained by his family following the marriage of one of his sons, William, to a daughter of Rhys ap Gruffyd.

Meanwhile the ruins of the abbey founded by Robert and his wife can be seen to this day and are a popular tourist attraction.

In a much later century and on the high seas, Admiral of the Fleet Sir George Martin was the distinguished Royal Navy officer whose lengthy service included the American War of Independence, the French Revolutionary War and the Napoleonic Wars.

Born into a naval family in 1764, he was a

grandson of Admiral of the Fleet Sir William Rowley, a great-nephew of Admiral Sir William Martin and a nephew of Captain – later Vice-Admiral – Joshua Rowley.

First entering naval service, aged only thirteen, aboard Joshua Rowley's ship HMS *Monarch*, he steadily rose through the ranks and was promoted to full admiral in 1821.

Serving as Vice-Admiral of the United Kingdom from 1834 to 1846 and knighted in 1837 for his service in so many theatres of naval warfare, he died in 1847 after having been promoted to Admiral of the Fleet; his sword is now held in the collections of the National Maritime Museum, Greenwich.

Chapter three:

Campaigners for rights

Instrumental in the foundation in the early nineteenth century of the Society for the Prevention of Cruelty to Animals (SPCA), was the Irish politician and animal rights' activist Richard Martin, nicknamed "Humanity Dick."

Born in 1754 at Ballyinch Castle, Co. Galway, he represented the seat of Jamestown in the Irish House of Commons from 1776 until 1783 and also served for a time as High Sheriff of Co. Galway.

In 1798 he was elected Member of Parliament (MP) for Lanesborough and, although raised a Protestant, argued vociferously for the cause of Irish Catholic Emancipation – this at a time when Catholics on the island were subjected to harsh penal laws.

With the passing of the Act of Union between Ireland and the rest of the United Kingdom in 1800 and the subsequent dissolution of the Irish Parliament, he was returned to the House of Commons in Westminster as MP for Galway as an Independent.

In addition for fighting for the cause of

Catholic Emancipation in Ireland, he also campaigned against animal cruelty – particularly the 'sports' of dog fighting and bear baiting, and the ill-treatment of carriage horses.

This resulted in 1822 in the passing of Martin's Act, officially entitled "ill Treatment of Cattle Act", while in 1824 he was present when the SPCA was founded in a London coffee shop.

Although he had been the prime mover behind the formation of the society, Martin modestly denied this.

A popular character – although he was often ridiculed in the pamphlets of the time for his tireless campaigning against animal cruelty, with one pamphlet depicting him with the ears of a donkey – he was a friend of many leading figures of the day.

Not least among them was King George IV – and it was he who bestowed on him the nickname "Humanity Dick."

In what now appears to have been something of a political set-up, most probably because of his support for Catholic Emancipation, he was accused of "election irregularities" and dismissed from the Commons.

Forced to flee to France with his family in

1826, it was here that he died in 1834 – with emancipation, to his great satisfaction, having finally been granted five years earlier.

He was married to the Anglo-Irish novelist and stage critic Harriet Evans Martin, whose many works include her 1788 novel *Dublin* and the 1802 *Helen of Glenross*.

She died in 1846, while she and her husband were the parents of the novelist Harriet Letitia Martin. Born in London in 1801 but raised at the family home in Ireland, she and her mother and another sister had followed her father into exile in France.

Later settling in Dublin, where she died in 1846, she penned a number of novels that include her 1835 *Canvassing*, while her cousin Violet Florence Martin and niece Mary Letitia Martin were also noted literary figures.

While Richard Martin was a prominent campaigner for animal rights and Catholic Emancipation, Selina Martin was actively involved in the early suffragette movement – the campaign for women to have the right to vote.

Born in 1882 in Ulverston, Cumbria, her commitment to the cause came at no small cost.

It was in Liverpool on December 20 of 1909

that she and fellow suffragist Leslie Hall approached Prime Minister Herbert Asquith as he was alighting from his car.

Berating him on the subject of women's rights, the Prime Minister chose to ignore them and, frustrated by his attitude Selina Martin threw an empty ginger bottle into the now empty vehicle.

Both women were immediately arrested and, with bail refused, remanded in custody for six days in the city's Walton Prison.

Protesting against their incarceration, the pair adopted the suffragette tactic of going on hunger strike.

The prison authorities, predictably, resorted to the tactic that they employed in such circumstances by having the women bound and shackled and force fed through the inhuman technique of administering the food through a nostril.

Brutally treated by their warders – who were, ironically, female – the two women were finally returned to stand trial on December 27.

Leslie Hall was sentenced to one month's imprisonment with hard labour and Selina Martin to two months.

Refusing to wear prison uniform and recommencing their hunger strike the pair were again subjected to brutal treatment that included not only being force-fed but confined to straight-jackets and placed in punishment cells.

Both women grew rapidly weaker, and it was not until February 3 that they were released.

The details of the treatment they had endured soon became widely known and caused a political storm.

The Home Secretary, Herbert Gladstone, however refuted the women's claims, stating that 'no unnecessary violence had been used and that they had made no complaint at the time.'

The date of Selina Martin's death is not known, but she would have been aged 36 when in February of 1918 the Representation of the People Act gave women aged over 30 the right to vote.

But it was not until ten years later that the franchise was extended, on the same terms as men, to all women aged over 21.

In contemporary British politics, Michael Martin, more formally known as Baron Martin of Springburn, is the Labour Party politician and former Speaker of the House of Commons born in Glasgow in 1945, the son of a merchant seaman and a school cleaner.

Leaving school when aged 15 to take up an apprenticeship as a sheet-metal worker, he later worked in the Rolls-Royce plant at Hillington and became involved in trades union activities.

Serving for a time as a Labour Party councillor on the former Glasgow Corporation, he was elected as MP for Glasgow Springburn in 1979 and served as Speaker of the House of Commons from 2000 until his resignation in June of 2009.

His resignation came as a result of a lack of both public and parliamentary confidence in his handling of the row over MPs' expenses.

He was created a life peer as Baron Martin of Springburn and sits in the House of Lords as a Crossbencher, while in the 2010 television film *On Expenses*, he was portrayed by fellow Scot Brian Cox.

Born in Edinburgh in 1954, David Martin is the Labour Party politician who has served as a Member of the European Parliament (MEP) since 1984 and as Vice-President of the Parliament from 1989 to 2004.

In Canadian politics, Paul Martin, born in 1938 in Windsor, Ontario, is the Liberal Party politician who served as his country's Prime Minister from 2003 to 2006.

Chapter four:

On the world stage

After being employed in a highly varied number of jobs that included delivering bootleg liquor, blackjack dealer, working in a steel mill and a brief career as a welterweight boxer, Dino Paul Crocetti became the American comedian, actor and singer better known as Dean Martin.

Born in 1917 in Steubenville, Ohio, to Italian-American parents, by the time he was aged 29 he was pursuing a career as a nightclub singer.

It was while performing in a New York club that he met the comedian Jerry Lewis, and the pair formed a popular musical and comedy act.

They performed together in a number of radio and television shows and films before Martin, nicknamed "King of Cool" because of his laid-back demeanour and easy singing style, became a top-selling recording star with hits that include *That's Amore*, *Everybody Loves Somebody* and *Little Old Wine Drinker Me*.

Host from 1965 to 1974 of the television variety programme *The Dean Martin Show* and, from

1974 until 1985 *The Dean Martin Celebrity Roast*, he
also starred in a number of films that include the 1959
Rio Bravo, the 1960 comedy *Who Was That Lady?* –
which won him a Golden Globe nomination for his
performance – and the 1965 *The Sons of Katie Elder*.

Also one of the members, along with fellow
entertainers and friends Frank Sinatra, Sammy Davis,
Jr., Joey Bishop and Peter Lawford, of what was
known as The Rat Pack, he died in 1995, the recipient
of three stars on the Hollywood Walk of Fame, while
he was also honoured with a posthumous Grammy
Lifetime Achievement Award.

In contemporary entertainment, Stephen
Glenn Martin is the multi-talented American
comedian, musician, actor, screenwriter and author
better known as **Steve Martin**.

Born in 1945 in Waco, Texas and the
recipient of a number of awards that include an
American Comedy Award, he is known for films that
include the 1970 *The Jerk* and, from 1987, *Roxanne*.

Known for her roles of Nancy Drew in the
television series *The Hardy Boys/Nancy Drew Mysteries*
and of Fallon Carrington Colby in the television soap
Dynasty, **Pamela Sue Martin** is the American actress
born in 1953 in Hartford, Connecticut.

In addition to her television credits, her big screen credits include the 1972 *The Poseidon Adventure* and, from 1974, *Buster and Billie*.

Known for his role of Morty Seinfeld, the father of Jerry in the popular sitcom *Seinfeld*, **Barney Martin** was the American actor and writer born in 1923 in Queens, New York.

A U.S. Army Air Force (USAF) navigator during the Second World War and later a detective with the New York Police Department, he entered show-business in 1955.

He died in 2005 with film credits that include the 1968 comedy *The Producers* and the 1981 *Arthur*.

Born in 1947 in Portland, Maine, **Andrea Martin** is an American actress, comedian and impressionist.

Winner of the Tony Award for Best Featured Actress in a Musical for her role in the 2013 Broadway revival of *Pippin*, her film credits include the 2000 *All Over the Guy* and the 2002 *My Big Fat Greek Wedding*, while she is also known for her comic impersonations of celebrities including Barbara Streisand and Sally Field.

Born in 1922, **Dick Martin** was the American comedian who co-hosted the ground-breaking comedy and variety television show *Rowan and Martin's Laugh-In* from 1968 until 1973; he died in 2008.

On British television screens, **James Martin** is the actor who, from 2004 to 2006, played the character Peter Beale in the soap *EastEnders*; born in 1992, his film credits include the 2003 *Kiss of Life*.

An English actress, singer, dancer and comedian **Jessica Martin**, born in 1962 in Fulham, London, was the 'voice' of the Queen in the satirical British television series *Spitting Image*, while she also provides the voice for Empyrea in the PlayStation2 game *Dragon Quest VIII*.

Born in 1972 in Malton, West Riding of Yorkshire, **James Martin** is the English celebrity chef who has appeared on a number of culinary-related television programmes.

At the time of writing he also holds the world record for chopping carrots – 515 grams in one minute – a feat achieved in aid of the Children in Need charity.

Born in 1934 in Romford, Essex, **Millicent Martin** is the English singer, actress and comedian best known for having been from 1962 to 1963 the resident singer on the television satire *That Was The Week That Was*, while she has also appeared in the American sitcoms *Frasier* and *Will and Grace*.

Behind the camera lens, Irwin Martin Cohn was the American television producer better known as **Quinn Martin**.

Born in 1922 in New York City, his many directing credits, from between 1959 and 1980, include *The Untouchables*, *The Fugitive*, *The Streets of San Francisco*, *Barnaby Jones* and *Cannon*.

The winner of two Emmy Awards for his work and a member of the Television Hall of Fame, he died in 1997.

Born in Liverpool in 1938, **Philip Martin** is the English television screenwriter whose many credits include *Z-Cars*, *Gangsters*, *Tandoori Nights* and, from 1992, *Virtual Murder*, in addition to writing *Dr Who* serials and episodes of *Hetty Wainthropp Investigates*.

Bearers of the Martin name have also excelled in the highly competitive world of sport.

On the fields of European football, **Bent Martin** is the Danish former professional goalkeeper born in 1943.

Winner of the 1960 Danish Championship

and the 1965 Danish Cup while playing for AGF
Aarhus, he joined Scottish club Celtic in February of
1966 but left to join Dunfermline Athletic in
December of that year, winning the Scottish Cup with
the club in 1968.

Later playing for Austrian club Rapid
Vienna, he ended his playing career in 1973.

He is the father of the Danish retired
badminton player **Camilla Martin** – also known as
Camilla Martin Nygaard – born in Aarhus in 1974.

Winner of the silver medal in women's
badminton singles at the 2000 Olympics, she is also a
winner of the World and All-England singles titles.

On the athletics track, **Ken Martin** is the
American former long-distance runner born in 1958.

A two-time United States national champion
in the marathon, at the 1985 Pittsburgh Marathon he
competed along with his then wife, **Lisa Martin**,
and they became the first married couple ever to both
win in their respective divisions.

His former wife, born Lisa Frances O'Dea in
Gawler, South Australia in 1960, and now known as
Lisa Francis Ondieki, won the gold medal in the
marathon in both the 1986 and 1990 Commonwealth
Games.

Her second marriage, which also ended in divorce, was to the Kenyan runner Yobes Ondieki.

An inductee of the Sport Australia Hall of Fame, she is also the recipient of an Australian Sports Medal.

From sport to the world of music, Christopher Anthony John Martin is the English singer, songwriter and multi-instrumentalist better known as **Chris Martin**, one of the founders of the band Coldplay.

Born in 1977 in Exeter, it was while studying at University College London – graduating with a first class honours degree in Latin and Greek – that he met future bandmates Guy Berryman, Jonny Buckland and Will Champion.

Coldplay was formed in 1996, and with Martin as lead vocalist, rhythm guitarist and pianist, the band has gone on to enjoy international success with hit singles that include the 2000 *Yellow*, the 2003 *Speed of Sound*, the 2008 *Viva la Vida* and the 2014 *A Sky Full of Stars*.

In 2002, Martin met the English actress Gwyneth Paltrow. The couple married a year later, but announced their separation in March of 2014.

On American shores, **Marilyn Martin**, born in Tennessee in 1954, is the American singer who, in addition to providing backing vocals for other artists who include Stevie Nicks, Joe Walsh and Tom Petty, has enjoyed solo success with hits that include her 1985 *Separate Lives* duet with Phil Collins.

Born in 1971 in Puerto Rico, Enrique Jose Martin Morales, better known as **Ricky Martin**, is the singer who is a major star in the Latin Pop genre, with hits that include *Livin' la Vida Loca* and *She Bangs*.

Known as "The Fifth Beatle" because of his early and close involvement with the band, George Henry Martin, more formally known as Sir George Henry Martin, is the acclaimed English record producer, arranger, composer, conductor and audio engineer more familiarly known as **George Martin**.

Born in 1926, it was after service during the Second World War with the Fleet Air Arm of the Royal Navy that he attended, from 1947 to 1950, the Guildhall School of Music and Drama.

He joined EMI Records after working for a time for the BBC's classical music department.

In June of 1962, the Beatles auditioned for him and, duly signed to a contract, the band went on to record a number of early hit singles that include

From Me to You and *Love Me Do* – all produced by Martin – as were a number of others that followed.

His many awards and honours include a 1964 Academy Award nomination for Scoring of Music for the Beatles film *A Hard Day's Night* and a 1967 Grammy award for Best Contemporary Album as producer of *Sgt. Pepper's Lonely Hearts Club Band*.

Honoured with both a CBE and a knighthood for his contribution to music and considered one of the greatest record producers of all time, other honours include induction into the Rock and Roll Hall of Fame, the UK Music Hall of Fame and, in 2002, the Lifetime Achievement Award for Services to Film by the World Soundtrack Academy.

He died in 2016.

From music to the world of the written word, George Raymond Richard Martin, better known as **George R.R. Martin**, and also as GRRM, is the best-selling American fantasy, science fiction and horror writer born in 1948 in Bayonne, New Jersey.

Winner of numerous awards that include a Quill Award and the British Fantasy Award, he is best known for his *A Song of Ice and Fire* series of novels – adapted for the television series *Game of Thrones*.

In a much different writing genre, **James Martin** was the British Information Technology (IT) consultant and author born in 1933 in Ashby-de-la-Zouch.

Nominated for a Pulitzer Prize for his best-selling 1977 book *The Wired Society: A Challenge for Tomorrow*, he died in 2004.

One prominent late seventeenth century author was the rather oddly named **Martin Martin**, born at Bealach, near Duntulm, on the Isle of Skye.

His date of birth is not known, but it is known that he died in 1719 and that it was in 1695 that he published his famous *A Description of the Western Isles of Scotland*.

A graduate of Edinburgh University and Leyden University, Martin was also a geographer and a mapmaker, and his monumental work on the Western Isles remains an extremely valuable source for researchers.